Brief Reviews for *Praying in the Zone*

Anyone interested in contemplative prayer will find these poems a starting point for deep reflection. They will not necessarily find quick answers to life's tough questions here, but rather observations framed in a stream of consciousness, full of awe, compassion, mystery, beauty, melancholy and paradox. They speak to different emotions, states of mind and circumstances - intensely personal yet universal in their relevance.
Jane Graham, WCCM meditator, Buckingham, England

Vernon Chandler's poems guide us in a spiritual effort that can resemble the work of digging. But attentive digging is much more than getting material out of the way and replacing it with a hole or a mound (or both). Things may look more or less the same after we have done the work of prayer—no hole, no mound, just a seemingly level surface. But look more closely, and you'll notice that the surface has been changed—watered and open, prepared to welcome a much deeper life.
The Rev. Craig A. Moro, retired clergy, Portland, Oregon

Vernon Chandler exercises the challenge of putting into words the mystical reality that by its own nature is beyond words. But he takes on this impossible task with genuine honesty, using a language that mixes struggle with institutional religion and wonder with nature and the spiritual presence in every second of life.
Leonardo Correa, WCCM meditator and WCCM director of communications, Porto Alegre, Brazil

Why do we eat sacred bread, yet remain hungry? Why do we dig so many wells, yet remain thirsty? What if our attempts to draw closer to God are the very things that prevent us from embracing the wonder, the awe, the stillness, the beauty, the mystery, and the love of the Divine already flowing in and through all of creation, and indeed at the center of our very being. What if prayer doesn't connect us to a Divine being somewhere else, but flows out of our oneness with the Divine Presence in us? In this collection, Vernon Chandler invites us to take off the training wheels of our religious words and encounter something more real than we ever imagined through the mystery of prayer.

The Rev. Dr. Craig J. Sefa, parish minister and author of *When Every Space Is Sacred: Cultivating an Awareness of God's Presence in Everyday Life*, Concord, North Carolina

Vernon's writings always touch a deep place within me. Perhaps that is because he invites us to look beyond the surface of things to the Reality beyond all things.

The Rev. Dr. Alexis Fathbruckner, retired clergy and Kindred Project community, Blackstone, Virginia

An inspiring meditation on the spiritual life! Through simple poetry, Vernon Chandler expresses the profound mysteries of faith, making that which is often unapproachable and complex . . . beautiful and engaging. These poems bring a fresh perspective into the meaning of prayer.

The Rev. Aristotle Rivera, U.S. Navy chaplain, Oxnard, California

Those who are familiar with Vernon Chandler's first collection of poems will not be disappointed with these new works, the fruit of his daily meditation practice. The images and insights expressed are the direct outflow from the wordless form of prayer which has become integral to his spiritual journey. Reflected in these remarkable poems is his own gradual awakening to the transcendent experience awaiting all spiritual seekers who have the courage to remove what he vividly terms "the training wheels" of dogma and doctrine which traditional Christianity has put on the soul's yearnings for a deeper relationship with the Ground of Being, and instead to trust oneself to the guidance of the indwelling Spirit. Once again, Vernon Chandler

inspires the thoughtful reader to strike out or to persevere on the spiritual adventure for which each of us was created.
Jean Dorband-Penderock, WCCM meditation group leader, Marburg, Germany

A beautiful collection that digs deep into the heart of spiritual mysteries, and captures the rhythms of life and nature. I love the way the author finds the sacred within the ordinary, mundane, everyday things, such as a roadside hand pump.
Vivien Proctor-Parr, WCCM meditator, Warwickshire, England

Powerful, emotive, sensitive, beautiful: simple words cannot express the wonder and feeling these poems evoke. I was captivated from the first encounter. Vernon takes you by the hand and gently leads you on a journey to your heart. I found this collection profoundly moving, staying with me and leaving me wanting more. Each poem is a gem to be treasured.
Julia Williamson, WCCM meditator, Hampshire, England

Vernon Chandler's writings reveal the secret of paradox by transcendence. This is the mystery to all true Love-Religion-Life, and Prayer.
Clive Shearer, WCCM meditator, Esperance, Western Australia

In this captivating volume of poetry Vernon Chandler opens up a prayerful space for the reader to encounter the mystery of the Divine. As a modern mystic, he offers fresh and startling images that lead us on a path of surrender to the Holy. I highly recommend this book to family, friends and anyone in search of deeper spirituality.
The Rev. Dr. Karen Hudson, retired clergy and spiritual seeker, Caswell Beach, North Carolina

Once again, Vernon Chandler has captured the struggle that so many of us experience in our quest to become more spiritual persons. The gift of these writings stimulates the mind and soul of the reader and often causes one to think, "How did he know that I have those same feelings?" A great work and worth the read!!

The Rev. Dan Rhodes, retired clergy, Dadeville, Alabama

Vernon expresses his thoughts and feelings in a deep and reflective way that leads to experiencing creation, hearing nature's voice, and to emotionally feel the warmth of life. In each poem, Vernon's words make us experience life as both protagonists and antagonists. With Praying in the Zone, *our conscience cannot rest.*

The Rev. Dr. Anibal Cruz Báez, U.S. Army chaplain, retired, Trujillo Alto, Puerto Rico

These simple yet profound poems each take one metaphor and mine the depths of human experience in relation to divine intimacy through that metaphor: a tree, flower bed, even a shiny new bicycle. "Surfing the Holy Spirit" captures the "vibe" of the entire collection, inspiring us to take risks, trust the unknown, and savor the moments of divine presence showing up in our everyday lives.

The Rev. Dr. Susan M. Hudson, retired clergy, spiritual director, author of *Spirited Voyager: A Memoir of Motherhood, Mission, and Ministry*, Southern Pines, North Carolina

I've really enjoyed reading these beautiful, thought-provoking poems. The more I read them, the more I appreciate them. The poems give glimpses of an unfolding, unfinished journey through life. They deal with an awakening, finding our way, sorrow, pain, regrets, forgiveness and healing, wonders of nature, questions, prayer and hope. For those "on the journey," a recommended book for the bookshelf.

Anita Finnigan, WCCM meditator, Dorset, England

The height and depth of these poems can take one on a roller coaster ride, be it at a grand amusement park or the County Fair - breathtaking.
Eileen D. Brennen, healthcare professional and Kindred Project community, Appomattox, Virginia

Through the use of vivid imagery and language alternatively spare and profuse, Vernon Chandler's poems are imbued with unresolved tension and an almost unbearable yearning that reflect life and the human condition. He courageously walks the narrow path of paradox by describing what is ultimately indescribable.
Michael Harrison, fellow pilgrim and meditator, Vienna, Austria

These heartfelt poems offer a dose of both wisdom and reality while challenging some of the very things we assume as fact. With language that provokes and illuminates the sometimes-delicate balance between the Creator and the created we are led deeper on our journey towards genuine intimacy. These poems remind us we can bring our whole self to prayer, meeting God with words or wordless knowing and resting in that loving union.
Barbara Atkinson, spiritual director & end of life doula, Durham, North Carolina

Once again, a really beautiful book. Not only is it thought-provoking, but it also touches my heart in a unique way, helping me see God in the unseen and hear God's voice in what I thought was silent.
Aileen B. Urquhart, author of *I Belong, The Animal's Christmas* and other children's books, Yorkshire, England

Vernon's collection of works is thoughtful, and each piece originates from a deep place within. His poetic collection is filled with strong resonance and meaning. More to the point,

*these offerings are meant to be spiritually thought-provoking,
and given time to simmer, so that their meaning and spiritual
fragrance may have time to develop and be explored
more deeply.*
**The Rev. Dr. Robin Moore, chaplain and spiritual
guide/director, Catonsville, Maryland**

*This collection of poems should be received as a spiritual gift
because they will help bring readers into connection with the
eternal spirit of life. Throughout our lives, we seek this
precious divine connection. Sometimes it is present,
sometimes ephemeral. This connection is present in every
poem. The poems, taken together, manage to bring the
meaning and purpose of our living, our very existence, into
spiritual focus. Written with such beauty and with such
elegant simplicity, they will be universally accessible to
anyone questing for the eternal spirit of life.*
John Eichrodt, retired Lycée professor, Riedisheim, France

*With love and grace, these poems awaken me to a difficult
and stirring truth. How hungry my soul is for the intimate
rhythms of "prayer in the zone" as I serve in the trenches of
constant temptation to externals as a pastor, coach and
spiritual director. Chandler's voice throughout these poems
is the Voice of invitation -- to rest, grounding, connection,
fierce honesty, reverence and true humility. I will treasure
these accessible and substantially evocative poems as
companions in my upcoming sabbatical and will delight in
sharing with many colleagues who, like me, need the balm of
the Presence who calls us to our true home. Thank you,
Vernon, for reminding us that the contemplative life
nourishes powerful Presence, not passivity!*
The Rev. Jacki Belile, local church minister, Chicago, Illinois

Praying in the Zone

Other Books by

Floyd Vernon Chandler

FIREWORKS, HAND DIPPED ICE CREAM,
LIVE BAIT AND JESUS SAVES

BEYOND the GRAVE: Love and Immortality

PONDERINGS: Reflections on the Stuff of Life

The Stare of the Flounder

Praying in the Zone

A Collection of Poetry

FLOYD VERNON CHANDLER

Praying in the Zone

Paperback ISBN: 9798861132152

Hardcover ISBN: 9798861168458

Imprint: Kindle Direct Publishing

Front cover artwork by KC

Cover design and formatting by Amnet Systems

*This collection of poetry is
dedicated to the wonderful people and spiritually
awakened souls I've come to know via the World
Community for Christian Meditation, Benedictine
Oblate community, Kindred Project community, and
the Wesleyan Contemplative Order.*

"Thou hast created us for Thyself, and our heart is not quiet until it rests in Thee."
Saint Augustine

"Through the study of books, one seeks God; by meditation and prayer, one finds God."
Padre Pio

"Prayer is not asking. It is a longing of the soul. It is daily admission of one's weakness. It is better in prayer to have a heart without words than words without a heart."
Mahatma Gandhi

"The Word is living, being, all verdant greening, all creativity. This Word manifests itself in every creature."
Saint Hildegard of Bingen

"All things must come to the soul from its roots, from where it is planted."
Saint Teresa of Avila

"Prayer is to religion what original research is to science."
Thomas Merton

"Belief consists in accepting the affirmations of the soul; unbelief in denying them."
Ralph Waldo Emerson

"The meditative journey is one that has to involve our total being, and it is the challenge that everybody who starts out on this journey should realize at the beginning. Every part of our life has to be transcended as we journey from the periphery to the center."
John Main

"But when you pray, go into your room, close the door and pray to your Father, who is unseen. Then your Father, who sees what is done in secret, will reward you."
Matthew 6:6 NIV

"Neither shall they say, Lo, here! or, there! for lo, the kingdom of God is within you."
Luke 17: 21

Table of Contents

Acknowledgements

My sincere appreciation to the family and friends who encouraged me with the writing of this collection. A special thanks to Barbara Atkinson, Jacki Belile, Loretta Benninghove, Carol BeVille, Eileen Brennen, Finley C. Campbell, David Canada, Joseph Chandler, Kate Chandler, Leonardo Correa, Alessandra Cortese de Bosis, Annette Crumpton, Anibal Cruz, Dora Ann Cueto, Jean Dorband-Penderock, John Eichrodt, Alexis Fathbruckner, Anita Finnigan, Kathy Gibbs, Jane Graham, Myrtis Greene, Michael Harrison, Steve Harter, Karen Hudson, Sue Hudson, Jeannie Ledford, Bruce Lugn, Sandy Mackey, David McLean, Robin Moore, Craig A. Moro, Vivien Proctor-Parr, John R. Pope, Aristotle Rivera, Dan Rhodes, Brenda Rosson, Craig Sefa, Clive Shearer, Hughlene Smith, Aileen Urquhart, Carroll Webber, Shirley Werts, and Julia Williamson.

Introduction

"We are not human beings having a spiritual experience. We are spiritual beings having a human experience."
— Pierre Teilhard de Chardin, Catholic Priest and Apophatic Theologian: 1881 – 1995

"Prayer is the bridge between our conscious and unconscious lives."
--Henri Nouwen, Catholic Priest and Theologian: 1932 – 1996

This is why I speak to them in parables: Though seeing, they do not see; though hearing, they do not hear or understand. In them is fulfilled the prophecy of Isaiah: "You will be ever hearing but never understanding; you will be ever seeing but never perceiving. For this people's heart has become calloused; they hardly hear with ears, and they have closed their eyes. Otherwise they might see with their eyes, hear with their ears, understand with their hearts and turn, and I would heal them." But blessed are your eyes because they see, and your ears because they hear.
-Matthew 13: 13 – 16 NIV

Cognitive or intellectual knowledge about "God" rarely brings spiritual awakening. For some of us, the intellect may hinder spiritual awakening and awareness.

A few folks, like Saul of Tarsus, have sudden epiphanies akin to his Damascus Road experience. For most of us, incorporating a discipline of contemplative prayer, or meditation, is the key to sensing the spiritual realm.

Prayer is an integral aspect of any spiritual discipline. Prayer includes all intentional spiritual practices which encourage the transcendent experience.

Without an active prayer life, academic theology remains hollow and social action is ineffective.

1

We never arrive on this spiritual journey. We are all beginners.

My ongoing spiritual awakening has benefited from the contemplative practice taught by the World Community for Christian Meditation (WCCM). It is a form of prayer that seems to work well with meditators from intuitive (apophatic) or sensing (kataphatic) spirituality temperaments.

I've been meditating for only two years. I am such a novice! This collection of poetry flowed from images and insights following daily meditations. I am appreciative of those in my meditation sharing group who helped give shape and form to several of these inner intuitions.

Most of these poems reflect an apophatic spirituality.

I hope some of these reflections resonate with you, the reader.

Vernon Chandler, Ansbach, Germany
August 4, 2023

SDG

Surfing the Holy Spirit

True prayer

Increases our mindfulness.

The Spirit manifests

Differently:

Nudges,

Dreams,

Synchronicities.

Sometimes

As ocean waves,

Filled with living water.

Catch the wave!

Allow the awareness,

Creativity,

Love,

Carry you toward shore.

Marvel as your soul

Glides as a surfboard

Propelled by Spirit.

Upon Awakening

As he slumbered,

The dream seemed so real.

He is awakening from it.

Was it sleepwalking,

Siesta talking?

What was he thinking?

Or was it a stupor,

Zombie-like existence?

Had he been

Half awake,

Partially asleep,

During most of this life?

AWAKE, AWAKE, AWAKE!

The day is ending.

Stream of the Unknowing

Invisible,

Unseen,

Unknowing,

Permeating life

As an underground stream.

Forever flowing;

Hidden,

As the ocean

In a wave.

Beyond words,

Defying logic.

Mystics experience it.

Religion attempts to capture the mystery.

Impossible!

Living water flows

Through and around

All attempts at ownership.

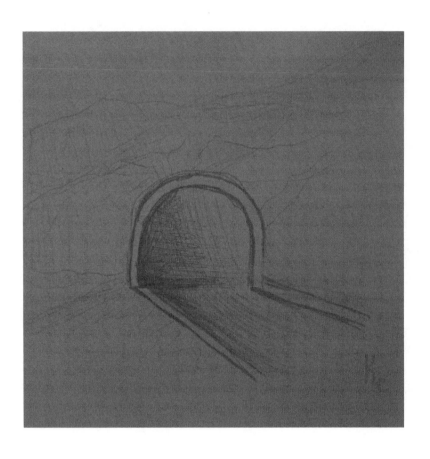

Unseen Tunnel

Entrances abound,

Everywhere!

Yet,

We stumble,

Half awake,

Half asleep,

Walking in circles,

Mistaking the illusion

For the real.

The tunnel,

More real than real,

Unseen,

Invisible.

Walls of faith;

Ambience of hope;

Radiant love

Flows

As an underground

Stream of Light,

Beckoning,

Whispering,

Nudging.

Stop,

Look,

Listen.

Entrances abound
Everywhere!
Closer than the air
We breathe:
Unseen tunnel.

Praying in the Zone

Is it left brain versus right brain?

Or does the left find harmony with the right?

Left brain praying is like using training wheels

On a bicycle.

Left brain praying focuses upon technique.

Left brain praying is cognitive,

Thinking.

Most religions teach left brain praying.

Real prayer transcends thinking.

Real prayer is beyond words.

Rituals, words, creeds are akin to training wheels.

The Spirit is beyond thinking.

Real prayer doesn't consist of lots of words and loud voices.

Many clergy and congregants think too much.

God is not asleep.

God doesn't need to be awakened by our prayers.

The Spirit never sleeps.

We are the ones who sleep,

Bumbling through our lives half awake,

Half asleep.

Wake up, Wake up!

Feel the wind!

Experience the flowing water!

Ride the ocean wave!

Glide down the snow-covered mountain!

Allow the Spirit to be with you in prayer.

Open your spiritual eyes.

Be here now.

This is the living water.

The Kingdom of God is all around us.

The Spirit is constant prayer,

With no beginning and no end.

Be silent and listen.

Cries from the Log Truck

I'm sure I heard their cries.

It was after dark.

The farming trucks could be heard

Miles away,

As a faint hum.

The volume increased as the trucks

Neared the Outlaws Bridge crossroad.

Some trucks carried squealing hogs and pigs,

Sentient creatures destined for slaughter.

The turkey and chicken trucks were quieter.

Birds roost in the dark.

It was their last night of life.

But then I heard the drone of a distant truck.

The sound suggested a heavy load.

The log truck came into view.

The freshly cut logs filled the attached trailer.

What remained of the trees' trunks

Were stacked lengthwise,

With a few small branches

Protruding from the sides,

Green leaves violently thrashing

In the wind

As the truck sped down Highway 111

For some distant lumber mill.

Was it right brain intuition?

I know I heard crying from the log truck.

Yes, the logs were crying.

The life force was still with them!

They were dying,

But not yet dead.

Who heard their moans of lamentation?

Many French headsmen claimed

The human head remained conscious

For up to twenty seconds

After the guillotine's blade fell.

I wonder how long a fallen tree remains aware?

The Shiny New Bicycle

It was a gift.

A shiny new bicycle,

With lights and bells,

Chrome colored fenders,

Padded seat,

Luggage carrier!

A real beauty!

It was the child's first bike.

For safety,

Temporary training wheels were added.

The child never removed them.

He rode that bicycle for years,

With training wheels attached.

The child worshipped those training wheels.

Religion was created to help point people to God.

Religion is akin to training wheels for the soul.

We often mistake religion for God.

Surrounded by Unknowing

In Hebrews it is written:
"Things which are seen are temporal;
Things which are not seen are eternal."
What is this ether
In which we move
And have being?
Unseen!
Unheard!
Unknowing!
Fish, reptiles
Sense infrared forms,
Invisible to you and me.
Dogs, elephants and dolphins
Hear ultrasound noises,
Silent to you and me.
What else remains hidden within
This cloud of unknowing?
Life is so precious;
Awareness so amazing.
Miracles abound!
The sacred permeates creation!
Religion attempts to confine
The Holy, the Unknown.
The Spirit defies to be captured.
The Holy cannot be seized.

Creeds, Rituals, Sacraments, Theology
Merely point to the Unknowing.
The Spirit is too awesome
For incarceration in religious prisons.

Bottles of the River Jordan

The vendors hawked

Empty plastic bottles

Alongside the Jordan River

Banks.

Each overpriced container,

Inscribed with the words,

"River Jordan from the Holy Land."

I bought two bottles,

Filling them with water

From the river's edge.

That was over twenty-five years ago.

The Jordan River water bottles

Rest among icons and votive candles
In a corner of my library.
Do I possess a few ounces,
Jordan River water?
Did the bottles capture
The flow, the current?
Is this living water?
No,
The Jordan River is not in my bottles.
So is it with religion and the Holy.
The Spirit cannot be put into a bottle.

Meditation as Well Digging

Digging a well
Begins with the
First shovel of soil.
Then another
And another,
Focusing upon
The shovel,
As the hole
Becomes
Deeper,
Deeper.

Rocks and stones
Distract the well digger.
Soil and clay
Change in color.
Digging feels endless.
No water.
Only dirt.
Another dry well?
Momentarily,
Thinking evaporates;
Well and shovel
Are forgotten;
Digging ceases.
Living water
Flows!

Wonder's Shadow

Dawn's early light
Reflected upon the ocean surface.
Vibrant yellow, pink, orange, blue
Interspersed among clouds and sky.
The hint and promise of sunrise.
Such awesome wonder!
The sight awakens the primordial.
Feelings of peace and calm
Touch the human soul.
Beneath the gentle and tranquil waves,
Morning horror begins again:
Feeding time for underwater creatures!
The hunter and hunted are the same.
Recently spawned life,
With eyes of innocence,
Curiosity,
Devoured
As breakfast meals.
Larger fish consume smaller ones,
Their stomachs mimicking
Matryoshka dolls.
Living sacrifices, everywhere.
Beginnings and endings.
Alpha and Omega.
Wonder is filled with

Life and death;
Joy and suffering;
Innocence and sin.
Meanwhile a disc of radiance
Rises over the endless horizon.
Rays of sunlight pierce the placid whitecaps.
Eating frenzy subsides.
Nautical Eucharist has ended.

Sin and the Peripheral

True prayer

Is

Centering,

Pulling and tugging,

The peripheral,

Closer,

Closer,

To the Center.

We orbit the Ground of Being,

Great Mystery,

Eternal Essence.

Sin is a peripheral creature,

Thriving in darkness,

Minimal gravity.

Without true prayer,

The orbit expands;

Peripheral becomes distant;

Spirit's pull lessens;

Desires and impulses strengthen;

Chatter replaces silence;

Self-will supplants Divine;

Spiritual eyes and ears close;

Sin glitters with false radiance;

Intoxicants further expand

Trajectory.

Like flood waters
Following a great storm,
Translucent waters
Hide multiple sins.
Murky waves,
Laden
With stupor and half wakefulness,
Push the peripheral further away,
Hiding entire villages of regret.
True prayer brings
Clarity.
Peripheral slowly recedes.
Sins emerge as
Center draws closer.
Spiritual awakening brings
Glimpses
Of the Center's brilliance,
Eternal love.
The ethereal light
Shines upon the soul;
Akin to the Sun,
Nearby planets.
True prayer
Tightens the orbit,
Restores sacred nudges and tugs.
The Master's words

"Thy will be done"
Carry deeper and deeper
Meaning.
Now we grasp
Immense hope,
Genuine sorrow,
As we plea,
"Forgive us our debts
As we forgive our debtors."

Impermanence

Look around.

Impermanence

Everywhere!

The faces,

Family,

Friends,

Neighbors,

Strangers,

Animals:

Future corpses,

Skeletons.

All life ends.

The birds of the air,

The creatures of the sea,

The snake,

The frog,

The mosquito,

The spider,

The flowering plant,

The majestic tree,

Await death!

What to do

While

Expending

Precious time?

We share this sacred space,

Together.

Recognize the impermanence.

Love is the essence,

From which all

Creation flows.

Love can't be captured,

Preserved.

Love can only

Be given,

Received,

As we await

Our destiny.

Silence and Prayer

Seeds do not sprout
Upon unplowed land.
Till the soil,
Using blade or plough.
Prepare the ground.
Patient stillness,
Advent time!
The miracle,
Mystery,
Unfolds unseen,
Beneath the surface.
New life bursts
Into sunlight.
Amazing wonder!
Silence,
Alone,
Isn't prayer.
Silence masks
Daydreaming.
Silence may conceal:
Pride,
Greed,
Anger,
Envy,
Lust,

Gluttony,

Sloth.

Silence becomes real prayer

When the quiet is

Tilled.

Contemplation,

Meditation,

Necessary

Spiritual ploughs

During silence!

Hide and Seek

Religious institutions,

Wonderful playgrounds

For Spirit!

So many places for

Hiding:

Creeds,

Rituals,

Doctrines,

Sacraments,

Music,

Stained glass windows,

Candles,

Incense.

The most secret place,

No one checks.

Walk over to the person

Nearby.

Look into their eyes;

Listen closely,

"Olly, Olly oxen free!"

I Am

Out of the burning bush,

"I am what I am."

The backside of I am,

An energy,

Glowing from human face.

The first commandment,

I am is the only I am.

Source of creation;

Spark of life.

Glimpses,

Mere glimpses,

Giving,

Receiving,

Surrendering,

Emptying,

Filling.

Flow is constant,

No beginning,

No end.

I am.

Votive Prayer Candle

Wax and a wick,

Nothing magical.

No séance or

Ouija Board.

No clandestine

Elixir.

Strike the match

And

Silently,

Reflectively,

Remember,

As the flame

Passes

From one to the other.

A visual icon,

Mantra of light,

Nucleus

For prayer.

The flickering glow,

Akin to beacons,

Focus

Our attention,

Guiding

Thoughts,

Loving energy,

Toward the soul.

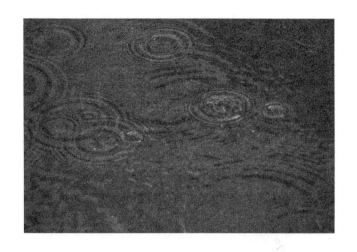

Ripples

Every pebble or stone;

Every word or action;

Creates ripples.

Miniscule waves,

Some small,

Others large,

Expand over the surface.

Hidden in darkness,

Visible in light.

Seen or unseen,

The movements felt

As spiritual karma.

Nothing remains concealed

Within the sacred realm.

Translucent Reflections

Science and physics
Study creation's complexities,
Intricacies.
Planets orbit around the sun;
Moons revolve around planets;
Galaxies consist of billions of suns.
In every atom,
Electrons move around a nucleus.
Ocean currents,
High and low tides,
Cyclones and hurricanes,
Powerful jet streams
Moving high
Above the Earth's surface.
Changing seasons
Mirroring
Birth,
Life,
Death,
Resurrection.
Every living cell,
Plant or animal,
Enthused by
Miraculous energy,
A life force,

Magic wand,

Transforming atoms

Into temporary

Living forms.

More awesome than

Created world,

The unseen.

Every wonder of the cosmos

Reflects even greater

Marvels,

Invisible.

Yet more real

Than real!

"For now we see

Through a glass,

Darkly!"

Like Grains of Sand

Like grains of sand,
Upon an endless beach,
My sins appear before me.
The Light pierces all darkness.
My wounds,
The wounded,
Interrelated,
Connected.
I seek
Forgiveness
From souls,
Living
And
Departed.
One precious life
Spent half-awake,
Half-sleep!
Has my Purgatory begun?
I look through my window
As through the bars of a prison cell,
Awaiting the day of judgement;
Trying to show kindness
To fellow inmates;
Hoping for forgiveness
As I forgive others.

The Mirage

What is real,

Really real?

Where does the illusion

Begin and End?

When do we awake

From the dream?

Is

Sight,

Sound,

Taste,

Smell,

Touch

All a mirage?

Is the hidden,

Unseen,

More real

Than real?

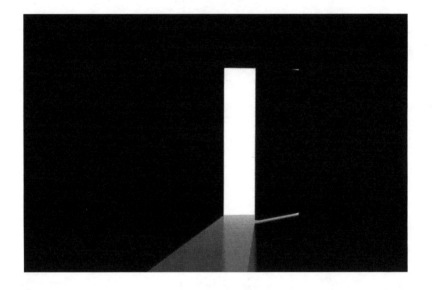

Please Help Me

The Spirit knows

Our every need.

No explanations,

Begging,

Reasons

Are necessary.

Divine Will be done,

On earth

As in heaven.

In our private room,

Behind closed door,

In the silence,

We wait.

Yet,

Sometimes the anguish,

Pain,

Sorrow

Overwhelms us.

We pierce the silence

With our cry,

"Help me!

Please help me!"

The Roadside Hand Pump

The metal contraption,
Simple to use,
Stood adjacent
To the highway.
The long pipe,
Mostly unseen,
Hidden,
Stretching deep
Into the ground.
A small pail of
Water at the base.
Priming the pump
Consisted of emptying
The bucket's fluid into
The shaft of the pump,
While rhythmically
Raising and lowering
The steel handle,
Up and down,
Up and down.
Initially
Nothing!
The spout
Remained dry.
Cars and trucks

Pass by.

Up and down,

Up and down.

Sounds are heard

Beneath the ground.

Up and down,

Up and down.

Suddenly,

Cool,

Fresh

Water

Flows!

Gallons and

Gallons!

An endless source!

Meditation,

A hand pump

For spiritual water!

Mantras help

Prime the pump.

Awakening to Hopeful Unworthiness

It is a bit like awakening from a long slumber,

This sudden glimpse of the spiritual realm

With infinite mystery and paradox,

Boundless and beyond comprehension.

Life is a miracle!

Existence is awesome!

What wonder surrounds us!

God, Tao, Christ, Allah, Oversoul,

Higher Power, Brahman,

Or is it beyond human words?

Creeds, dogmas, doctrines, rituals

Are outer shells,

Signposts to what

Is incomprehensible.

A constant emptying begins,

A surrendering that never ends.

Is it love, or something more?

Conviction and repentance are real

And painfully felt

As forgotten and unknown sins surface,

Emerging into consciousness

As bitter water

From a murky artesian well.

There is no going back.

Though we might try

To forget,

Or numb,

The ache.

Akin to peeling a pungent onion,

After one layer of tears

There is another and another

And another.

Remorse, regret, shame!

Does it ever end?

It is now so clear,

Or is it?

Fruits of the spirit?

Fruits of the flesh?

We seek

Forgiveness, forgiveness, forgiveness!

But forgiveness and forgiving are

Intertwined

And never complete.

Some say the scarlet becomes whiter than snow.

He doesn't know.

The crimson is now pink.

Or is it?

Red stains remain

And stubbornly cling,

Shouting unworthiness.

Is this contrition?

Or moral injuries

Without any cures?

The beginning of Purgatory

Or the paradox of faith?

The story of the Pharisee

And the tax collector

Gives him hope.

Immortality

Is the ocean in a wave?

When the waves cease,

The ocean remains.

Does the lowly caterpillar,

Weaving its shroud-like cocoon,

Have any inkling

Of what lies ahead?

From a tiny seed,

A giant oak tree grows;

But the shell of the seed

Must die

For new life to emerge.

Hidden in winter's death,

The hint of spring.

Nature shouts the choreography,

Life, death, and rebirth.

Death is the great mystery,

Life the amazing miracle,

Veiled in Mystery,

Paradox.

True Prayer

Go to your inner room

And close the door.

Many words

Are needless

For the Unseen

And Unknowable.

No words

Are required.

True prayer

Brings light

To darkness;

Focus and clarity

To vision;

Sight to

The Blind;

And hearing

To the Deaf.

Wonder

And awe

Surround us.

Miracles abound.

Please Forgive Me

Please forgive me.

Yes, you,

Reading these words.

I must tell you.

Please, listen to me.

I am sorry,

Genuinely sorry.

I have greatly sinned,

In my thoughts,

In my words,

In my deeds.

I apologize, to you,

Yes,

You,

For what I have done,

What I failed to do,

Through my fault,

My grievous thought.

I ask your forgiveness.

Please forgive me.

They Reappear

First,

They disappear.

Family and friends

Vanish!

Gone from our sight.

We mark departures

With flowers,

Eulogies,

Grief.

So final.

Then silence,

Utter quiet,

Long stillness.

No bridge exists.

Only memories

Planted,

Somewhere

In our heart.

Time passes.

Unexpectedly,

Akin to Emmaus,

They reappear,

Unrecognizable,

Mysteriously.

We sense the energy,

The love.

Trapdoors

Appearing as flooring,

Structurally sound,

Solid:

Creeds, rituals, doctrine, sacraments.

Important,

Concrete,

Inviting.

Yet,

Meditate closely,

Silently.

Feel movement.

Trapdoors

Opening,

Mysteriously.

Hidden passageways

Within the flooring:

Secretive as

Water in the sea,

Light from the sun,

Ocean in a wave,

Song from a bird,

Colors in a rainbow.

Bottomless.

Vastness

Beyond words.

Source of All,

Ground of Being.

Eternal

Pulsating love.

Trapdoors,

Waiting.

Knock,

They will be opened

To you.

Unseen

Energies and forces,

Unseen,

Surround us,

Often subtle,

Sublime.

Sometimes eerie,

Threatening.

Rhythms vary.

Sometimes distant,

Sometimes so close!

Imagination,

Fantasy,

Or

Otherworldly?

The unreal,

Invisible,

More real

Than

What we call

Real!

Taking Away the Sins of the World

It made no sense.

Wishful thinking,

Childish make-believe.

Does it even exist?

To err is human,

Isn't it?

Upon awakening

We discover.

It is real,

So very heartbreaking,

Painful,

Heavy.

What is the cure,

Remedy?

Is it like

Removing dirty plates from

A diner's table?

Or

Washing the stained clothes

After a laborer's toil?

No, it seems more akin

To a river's constant flow,

The rising and setting of the sun,

Moon,

Stars.

It is!

Don't try to think,

Analyze,

Or reason.

It has many names

And no name.

No beginning,

Or end.

Wade into the water.

See the light.

Feel the love.

The current never changes.

Ever giving,

Emptying,

Cleansing,

Forgiving,

Healing,

Eternal.

Weeds and Wheat

How did evil make an entry?

Was it sublime or profound?

Evil wears many masks!

Is it Ego versus Spirit?

Or does evil transcend human thought,

A paradox in creation?

A shadow that follows us

From birth to death?

Upon awakening,

Weeds become apparent.

How did we mistake

Weeds for wheat?

Holiness and evil,

Yin and yang.

No perfect wheat fields.

Weeds always emerge.

Beware of perfect wheat fields!

The Sacred Realm

It is akin to colorblindness,

Inability to sense the sacred.

The material realm seems so real!

The secular adorned with intelligence!

Saul had an epiphany.

Most of us lack Damascus Road awakenings,

Occasionally,

Sensing a glimpse,

But quickly discounting it all.

A spiritual realm:

Illogical,

Anti-scientific,

Wishful thinking,

Childlike,

Opiate for the masses.

Real prayer dissolves the material

Illusion.

Cracks appear,

Crevices open

Allowing the hidden and unseen

Expression.

Dormant seeds sprout.

Living water oozes from the ground.

The sunglasses lose their tint.

Scales fall from our eyes.

The secular was all façade.

Doctrine and dogma are for religion.

Spirituality and faith

Flow from the sacred.

Sounds in Silence

How did we not hear?

Energy, energy

Everywhere!

All creation

Permeates

Energy.

Before awakening,

Deafness.

Now,

Celestial orchestra.

Trees speak.

Rocks murmur.

Stars sing.

Energy exposes

Human word

Betrayal.

Trust the energy.

Listen with your heart.

Energy never lies!

Dress Rehearsal

Contemplative prayer
Brings one
To death's door.
Do not fear.
Death is not the end.
Only the illusion,
The material realm,
Is mortal.
The unseen,
Hidden,
Eternal.
Every meditation,
A dress rehearsal
For dying.

Our Spiritual GPS

A Global Positioning System

For the soul?

It seems to exist.

Regardless of the wrong turns,

Distance traveled,

The sins,

Or how lost we feel.

It signals,

Beckons,

Recalculates,

And

Redirects,

With nudges,

Hunches,

Coincidence.

Sometimes

Demanding

Attention.

Flowing

With never-ending

Grace,

Love,

Forgiveness,

Compassion!

It's tuned

To the heart,

Calling us home.

Annulment of Sin

When we awaken,

Sins appear;

Akin to poor grammar,

Misspelled words,

Hauntingly scribbled

Upon life's pages.

Is there an eraser?

A possible annulment?

Is a clean slate

Possible?

David recalled

Lust for Bathsheba,

Betraying Uriah.

Apostle Paul:

Saul of Tarsus,

Killer of believers,

Pharisee of Pharisees!

Saint Augustine:

Sexual immorality,

Manichaean religion years.

Annulment doesn't

Exist!

But,

Hope reigns eternal!

Bathsheba birthed

Solomon

Without whom

There would be no

Apostle Paul

Or Saint Augustine.

Within the oyster,

Analogous to sin,

The ineradicable,

Not annulled.

Mollusk contrition,

Penance,

Becomes the pearl.

Mantra of the Tree

Within deciduous trees,

Spiritual truths

Revealed.

Rain brings

Life to barren seed.

The color of Ordinary time

Creates energy from light.

Illusion of autumn death,

Winter's hint of rebirth,

Resurrection in spring.

Every leaf, a legacy.

The cycle repeats.

Beneath the surface,

Stillness,

Silence,

The unseen.

Roots go deep,

Tapping living water.

The Modern Dilemma

The anointed one said,

"No one can serve two masters:

For either you will hate the one,

And love the other;

Or else you will hold to the one,

And despise the other.

Ye cannot serve God and mammon."

This spiritual truth

Transcends religious traditions.

In houses of worship,

People seek

Sacred food;

Yet,

Remain hungry,

Wondering why.

The Flower Bed

It was confusing.

The child was young,

Maybe five or six.

One of his first

Childhood chores,

Saturday mornings,

Spring and summer,

Helping his Mom

Pull weeds from her flower bed.

Weeds look so similar to flowers.

Some weeds had flowers!

What had the weeds done,

That was so bad?

Did the weeds know

Not to grow in the flower bed?

Every week,

Weeds returned.

Pulling weeds was never ending!

But with time,

The child recognized

Differences

Between weeds and flowers.

Prayer is a similar teacher,

Helping discern

Sin and holiness.

The Play Park

Human life,

A children's playpark!

Sliding board beginning;

Swing set a favorite,

First with pushes,

Later with arms,

Back,

Legs.

How high can you go?

Merry-go-round

Disorientation;

Playhouse

Imaginations;

Teeter Totter

Ups and downs;

Monkey bars,

Frightening at first!

We keep coming back,

Climbing new heights,

Swinging

Upon the horizontal ladder.

Toward the end of the day,

We hang by our hands,

Prayerfully pondering

When to let go.

Preaching

Sermons are difficult,

Next to impossible

When minister

Lacks prayer life.

Words,

Only words,

Sounding from the pulpit,

Echoing,

Ricocheting off walls,

Ceiling,

And floor,

Especially tough when

Congregants have

No prayer life, too!

Surfaces

Deflect

Words,

Distract

Meaning.

Sunday morning

Peripheral

Chatter,

Daydream time,

Break from television.

Checking watches,

Waiting for coffee and fellowship.

I

What is the

I?

Might I

Relate to eye?

Perception

Impacts

I,

Doesn't it?

Is mind's eye,

I?

Is I,

Ego?

Spirit?

Evil?

Good?

Neither?

Perhaps location matters.

Peripheral I?

Or

Centered I?

Like gravity,

Prayer pulls

I,

Away from the fringes,

Toward the center.

Theology

Theology schools galore!

Lectures!

Research papers!

Books!

Books!

Books!

"So much straw,"

Saint Aquinas concluded.

Without prayer life,

Religion,

Empty;

Sermons,

Lifeless;

Theology,

Hollow.

Save the World

You want to save the world?

First,

Save yourself!

Peripheral energy:

Angry,

Anxious,

Fearful,

Frantic.

Centering energy:

Calming,

Healing,

Restoring,

Saving.

Social action

Without prayer life:

Ineffective,

Dangerous.

Refreshing water,

Pure love,

Flows outward

From the center.

The world is in

Constant need of saving.

Please save oneself

Before saving others.

Shells

Shells,

Shells,

Everywhere!

All creation,

A shell,

Concealing Divine energy.

The material plane

Shrouds the Eternal.

Teilhard observed,

"We are spiritual beings

Having a human experience."

But,

So are all living things!

Animals, Birds, Fish,

Flowers and Trees,

Every insect:

Spiritual beings

Having life form experiences.

With prayer,

Miniscule cracks appear,

Allowing glimpses,

Of the Sacred,

Hidden,

Beyond the shells.

Skipping Stones

It is akin to skipping stones

Across the surface of the water.

Words!

Knowledge!

Theology!

Minor ripples distort

The sun's reflection.

Six skips, seven,

Maybe eight?

Smooth stones,

With strong arms,

Sometimes reach the other side,

Never sinking to the

Depths.

Light pierces the water's external illusion,

Prayer provides underwater glimpses,

Stones slowly descending,

Going deep,

So very deep.

Faith,

Hope,

Love.

The deepest is Love.

Time

The Eternal One

Named,

"The light,

Day;

Darkness,

Night."

Life forms

Mark memories by

Mornings,

Evenings,

Lunar phases,

Seasons.

Could a squirrel use a watch?

A rooster an alarm clock?

How does a salmon

Know when to spawn?

Or

Snow geese

Fly south?

Flowers blossom?

Oak trees form acorns?

Does the riverbed

Perceive time?

Early timepieces,

Neither minutes or seconds!

Sundials measured hours,

Varying in length,

Longer in summer,

Shorter in winter.

Time zones did not exist

When California became a state.

Jet lag was unknown.

Now appointments,

Train schedules,

Airplane departures,

Bus stops,

Even worship services

Adhere to precise hour and minute.

Artificial numbers

Displayed upon clock face,

Smartphone screen.

We borrow an hour in Spring,

Returning it in Fall,

Calling it Daylight Savings Time.

Nature must find it amusing.

Prayer beckons,

Meditation reveals:

Sacred,

Timeless,

Eternal

Center.

Meditation

The sky is dark,

Pitch black.

Rain falls,

Sheets of

Gray-colored auroras.

Fog rises

From the pavement,

Creating ghostly

Apparitions.

Narrow shoulders

Slope along the road.

There are

Curves,

Potholes.

Meditation,

Our windshield wiper

In the stormy night

We call life.

Darnel and Oxbow Lakes

The anointed one observed,

"Though seeing,

They do not see;

Though hearing,

They do not hear."

From the fringes,

Sin appears disguised,

Camouflaged,

Harmless.

Darnel appears

As wheat;

Oxbow lakes:

Flowing river.

The peripheral,

Akin to the carnival's

House of Mirrors,

Distorted images

Everywhere!

Speakers blare

Competing noises;

Sounds of

Feigned laughter

Echo along

Glass walled

Corridors.

Busyness,

Aimless chatter,

Cheap grace,

Permeate

Far and wide.

True prayer tugs

One inward,

Away from the secular orbit,

Toward the center,

Source of Light,

Love;

Emptying,

Receiving,

Giving;

Gifting eyes

With sight,

Ears with understanding;

Exposing the bizarre,

Evil;

Weeds appear

Among wheat;

Stagnant water

Alongside

Living streams;

Akin to awakening

From a meaningless

Dream.

About the Author

Vernon Chandler follows the daily discipline of meditation as taught by the World Community for Christian Meditation (WCCM). He considers the WCCM his spiritual home. Vernon has made first vows as a Benedictine Oblate.

Prior to discovering the WCCM, Vernon provided 44 years of ministry in various parish and chaplaincy settings. He served for over 32 years, active and reserve, in the United States Army chaplaincy with foreign tours of duty in Albania, Bosnia, Bulgaria, Croatia, Germany, Hungary, Japan, Korea, Kosovo, and North Macedonia.